I'm Not Crazy

Timothy Jackson

SheEO
PUBLISHING COMPANY

I'M NOT CRAZY
Copyright 2015 Timothy Jackson

Published by SheEO Publishing
Locust Grove, VA 22508
www.AriSquires.com

Cover by SheEO Publishing, Locust Grove, VA
Cover Photo © Timothy Jackson

This book contains stories in which the author has changed people's names and some details of their situations in order to protect their privacy

Timothy Jackson Ministries
www.tdjacksonministries.org

ISBN-13: 978-0692385968

Acknowledgements

First and foremost I would like to thank God for the opportunity to share what he has given me with you.

I would like to thank my wife, Sandra, for her support and understanding while working on this book. I am grateful for her support and know how blessed I am to have her.

I would like to thank my children Timothy Jackson II and Sade Younger for their prayers and support since day one.

Thank you to the members of Trinity Fellowship International Church North and South for believing in me. I am grateful for your prayers. I don't take it lightly nor take it for granted.

My sincere thanks to Pastor Charles Wormley, who took time to mentor me as a young Christian. I learned a lot and I am passing it on. To the other great men of God who have encouraged and inspired me, thank you for sowing into my life.

A very special thanks to my many supporters, family, and friends. Your contributions and support during this process has not been taken lightly nor for granted.

Gratitude, thanks for financial support

Tina Davis, Prophetess Filmore Lorett, Sis Victoria Crenshaw, Sister Maggie Whitehead, Ray Lewis, Cheryl and Brian Roberson, Carla Minor, Howard & Cindy Nelson, Alger & Yvonne James, Damian Nelson, Rodney Robbins, Drea & Eugene George, Darryl Graham, Diriki Lewis, Joe and Dawn Smith, Vivian & Bernard Barber, Damian Nelson, Latan Fairchild, Janet Allen, Martha Williams, Jackie & Keith Armstead, Cecelia Andrew, Shawn Johnson (Junior), Eric Dyson (quiet storm), Mike & Alice Warren, Brian & Cheryl Roberson, Roosevelt Mcphail, Vicky, Sophia, Erika and Elizabeth Owusu, Ginger Thomas, Virginia Lyn, Michelle Edwards, Mike Boggs, Phyllis Hinton, Jackie Hail, Dinah Kirkland, Reggie Johnson, Nygel White, Evangelist Williams, Glendale Kirkland, Peggy Shankin, Monica Johnson, Shante Johnson, Carolyn Wilson, Cindy Burnside, Willis Frye, Mary Lumphine Benitez, James Peyton, Loraine Frye Washington, Peggy Ann Sharklin, James E. Peyton, Kennedy Dixon, Cynthia Burnside, Pastor William Frye & First Lady Frye, Rev. Nathan Crisp, Elmira Johnson, Sheona Williams, and Jeffy Lewis.

Foreword

I count this among my greatest honors to be asked by "Timmie" to share with him in this great achievement in his life, the publishing of the beginnings of his memoirs. *"I'm Not Crazy"* takes us from southeast DC, to a sleepy hollow fifty miles to the South, in Fredericksburg, VA; but the distance although few in miles, became a life time in difference.

As Tim's Pastor, I share in his adult Christian journey and his walk with the Lord and continue to do so in humble appreciation of what God continues to do in his life. I know his wife Sandra and their children Sade and Tim Jr., as they read this book will know most assuredly that it took the loving God of the universe to change their husband and dad into what he has become today, a gentle giant. So be my guest, join me and countless others as we look into the life of a Soul, a man, a depraved human vessel, once on the brink of despair, but snatched from the jaws of destruction and death by the sure hand and God and deposited into the Lamb's Book of Life.

Great work Tim, continue your journey with the Lord, because as they say He's not through with you yet!

Your friend, mentor and father in Ministry,

Charles W. Wormley
Sr. Pastor

Contents

Preface

TRANSFORMATION – I KNEW JESUS, BUT DIDN'T REALLY KNOW JESUS

Whenever my money would get low, I had a relationship with a friend of mine where I could go over to his house without calling. One afternoon I swung over to his house, and there were two vans with tinted windows sitting in front of the house. I had an eerie feeling, but I didn't pay it any mind and proceeded to go up to his house anyway.

It is very scary for me to share my experiences with you, and also extremely painful, but what I've learned is that it is also necessary for balance in my life. It is therapeutic as well and in the process of sharing, my burdens have been lifted.

As I was going towards his driveway, I heard somebody say, "Hit the ground, hit the ground now!" Then I heard *click, click, click, click,* which sounded like rifles. I have to be honest, I hit the ground real hard on my stomach, and I cried like a baby. I feared for my life.

Then, men seemed to come out of nowhere and everywhere at once—from the bushes, the cars, the back of the house. I felt them going in my pockets and heard them talking to each other. They told me to turn on my back so they could talk to me.

One asked me, "What are you doing here?"

I said, "I'm just here to see a friend, that's it."

"What are you over here for? Who do you know?"

"I'm just here visiting my friend, that's all."

"How often do you come here?"

"I just—he's my friend—I just come over every so often."

Then, they asked me if I had any money in my pockets. "No, I don't have anything."

They told me, "Don't ever come here again. Get out of here. Your friend is getting arrested."

I found out later that they were ransacking his house—he was in there and they had him waiting inside in handcuffs.

I drove all the way home, crying and all, just praying to the Lord, terrified and in shock.

Once I got home, I asked the Lord, even though I didn't really have a relationship with Him at this time, I asked Him to get me out of this one and I would never do it again.

What is so strange to me is realizing the fact that when I used to make the drug money, it seemed like it always came through when we really needed it. My wife and I would say this funny thing, "He's looking out for us," but we didn't really have a relationship, per se, with Him.

I always knew Jesus in my life; I just didn't always really *know* him in my life.

I had so many incidents that I ignored, or didn't quite understand, until He showed me that He was real.

Do not let your hearts be troubled. Trust in God; trust also in me.

(Jesus Christ)

After the incident with my friend's house being raided by the FBI, I went home, and allowed the truth of what happened to my friend sink in deeply. This started the transformation of me getting things together. My wife and

I agreed that we were going to have to do something. I bought a newspaper and began the search for someplace better. We finally saw a place down in Fredericksburg, VA, her hometown, and we put a deposit on it.

Within a couple of weeks we moved, but I was still going back and forth to Washington, DC, to hustle because the money I was making working a 9-5 wasn't what I was used to.

I would collect a lot of stuff, and I would give it to my kids, sell it, whatever the case may be. It got to the point when we moved, I was drinking beer and smoking herb, and my kids never wanted for anything. Every day seemed like it was Christmastime for my kids. They would wake up and I would have a new TV, clothes, beds, whatever I thought they needed waiting for them.

The enemy—the devil—he said to me, "You know, you can go up the road, do your herb, come down here and live clean and no one would ever know it at all."

And I said, "Well, that does sound really good."

And then the Lord spoke to me, "You already know what happens when you deal with him." He said, "Try me, try me."

When I heard that, I told my wife—she was my girlfriend at the time—that we were going to have to find a church to go to.

WE FINALLY WENT TO CHURCH

My wife called her brother to ask what church we could go to. He told her about a Baptist church in Fredericksburg, and we set out early but couldn't find it. It was getting late—it was almost 11:30 a.m.—so we ended up going to another one down the street.

We pulled into the parking lot and I said, "This must be a dead church because there's nobody here. The parking lot isn't full at all."

She said to me, "What do you want to do? Do you just want to go home and find the other church next week?"

"Well, since we're here, we'll go in."

So that was my mindset—that it takes a lot of cars to make a church. We went inside, and I remember the preacher was preaching, and then he said at the end of service, "What does it take for you to come to Jesus? Does it take the choir singing your favorite song?" And then he said, "Does it take the parking lot being full?"

Once he said that, I didn't see the preacher anymore—I saw and heard the voice of God. By this time, I was used to the voice. When he said that, the Lord showed me some past experiences.

He said, "Remember when the FBI man had a gun at your head and then the knock at the door, and you were able to escape? That was me that knocked at the door that allowed you to escape."

He said, "Remember you were so drunk and you walked out into the street, and you were so close to getting hit? The guy grabbed you so you wouldn't get hit in the street." He said, "I was that guy that grabbed you from behind."

He started showing me incidents where He actually saved my life, and He said, "If you don't accept me this time, I'm no longer coming to you again." And I believed that.

So I went to the front of the church, and I said, "I want Jesus, and I want this right now." The clerk there said, "Yes, yes you can accept Him right now."

I remember going to church from time to time where it's like a Band-Aid. When you're in trouble, you get straight, and then you leave the church and don't come back anymore. I said, "Lord, I don't want to do that this time. I want to stay with you. I don't want you to leave me, and I don't want

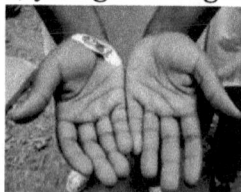

to leave you." He truly came into my heart that day. It was like a light bulb came on in my mind.

It was intriguing because after that day I couldn't watch TV the same way. The things that I used to do, I stopped immediately. My kids said, "Hey, you don't cuss anymore." I didn't even know He took cussing away from me. I got heavily fixed in his Word, really wanting to know more about Him, wanting to get closer to Him. I will forever remember the date, the time, the place—it was on June 25, 2005, at 12:30 p.m. That's when my life totally changed.

> When you are able to share your life experiences a lot of burden will be lifted off of you.

When you encounter God Himself, you will never be the same.
—Timothy Jackson, Pastor, Trinity Fellowship International Church

Introduction

For the early years of my life people called me crazy. Not the kind of crazy that was good, where I made people laugh and everyone liked being around me, but the kind of crazy that lowered my self-esteem, caused mental strain, depression, and isolation.

You will read about my journey of overcoming what other people thought I was, to who I became as a man of God. It wasn't one thing that changed my life from no direction to complete guidance. It was a series of lessons, revelations, encounters, and conversations that led to my faithfulness and happiness.

God gives us our strength—the good, the bad, and the ugly. We as believers have to trust that God knows what he is doing. He makes no mistakes.

My journey wasn't pretty. I did a lot of bad things to good people. I have forgiven myself and so has my Father.

As you read, *I'm Not Crazy*, I pray that my life experiences will resonate with you in some way, and that you will walk away after reading with a determination to know that you are not limited and that anything is possible with God, because you, me, he, she...we're not crazy.

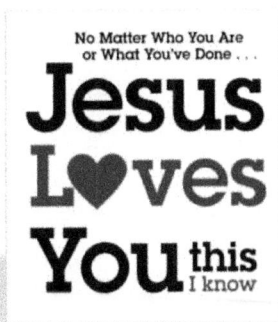

No Matter Who You Are
or What You've Done . . .

Jesus
L♥ves
You this
I know

I'm Not Crazy

CHAPTER ONE

The Demon in Me

"No," Jesus said, "I'll have no demon in me.
For I honor my Father-and you dishonor me."
John 8:49 NLT

Something happened to me when I was about five years old. See, I used to have this nickname Big M, which I took to heart. I say that because Big M was short for Big Mack and being identified as this relentless daredevil made me believe that I had to be tough, like I had to prove myself all the time. I even went so far as to think that I had to be better at being tougher than others.

One summer afternoon on the southeast end of Washington, DC, where I grew up as a child, the neighborhood kids challenged me to do a no-hand forward flip running down the hill. Being the bad to the bone kid I thought I was, I took the challenge. I did a no-hand front flip in the grass running down the hill. I landed on the top of my head instead of the bottom of my feet, and cut my head wide open. I don't remember much, but I do recall the blood blinding me because it was running so quickly down my face.

I also remember my mom screaming even though I could only see her a little bit. She was crying so badly and I believe she was paralyzed from shock to where she couldn't come to me as I was screaming out from agony. My aunt, I believe, was the one who came to me and wrapped a cold towel around me. Then I was taken to the hospital. As they were rushing me to the hospital, the EMTs were preparing for my head to be stitched closed.

Ever since that day, as I was growing up, up until at least fifteen years old, I vividly remember banging my head against the wall for no reason I can comprehend. It wouldn't be just a regular wall either, even though any wall is hard, but I remember banging my head against brick walls, sidewalks, it didn't matter, I would just bang my head.

I had a complex at an early age. A lot of people seemed to think and act like they were a lot brighter than me. They would make fun of me for every little thing I did. I couldn't do anything right in their eyes. So, I started not to like people. I treated everybody wrong, even my family.

I don't remember a whole lot during this time of my life, but I do remember the psychiatrist telling my mom, "Try not to get him upset," and "Treat him like he's normal."

As a child, I would get these really bad headaches every summer. I couldn't stand them, and nothing would take the pain away. Maybe it was the heat, but I believed they were so awful in the summer months because my mind would psychologically take me back to that disastrous stunt.

There was not any medicine, any sleep, or anything that would relieve my throbbing pain. I used to put a pillow around me at night, but the pain wouldn't go away. It was this constant pounding, this aching feeling that got in the way of my natural thoughts and me enjoying my childhood. The pain was like a reminder of what happened when I was a five.

Life was pretty uncomfortable and challenging. I didn't know what was going on. I didn't know who to talk to. I was in special education classes pretty much throughout my whole school career. Everybody called me crazy and retarded. I couldn't change them and I couldn't stop them. The more that they called me crazy, the more I acted like I was crazy.

I was about 12 or 13 when I started experimenting with drugs. Growing up in Washington, DC, in the 70s, drugs were everywhere and easy to get. Being the daredevil, I would try anything the kids at school offered me. It never really mattered to me what it was, as long as I was high. However, the reprieve was temporary as my head started ringing right after I would come down from my high.

Drugs had me bad. Since I was doing drugs at school, I would hardly pay attention. I was physically present, but not really present. One afternoon I just nodded my head down, fell to my left, and hit the floor because I had passed out. I don't even remember that whole day specifically, but I do remember I was sent to the school nurse and she just assumed I was ill. They never found out I had a drug addiction. They just thought I was crazy.

All of these little occurrences led up to me being challenged to do a lot of ruthless stuff. I used to blame it all on the alcohol and drugs because I didn't want to face the fact that I had real serious issues.

LIVING WITHOUT A DAD

I never knew him and don't know anything about him or he and my mother's relationship. I don't know if they were in love or even friends. I used to ask my mom about my dad, and she always said, "Hush up," and never gave me any answers.

Since I didn't have a father, I felt like everybody around me always looked down on me because they constantly said, "You will never amount to anything." Hearing this all day all the time made me want to take my insecurities and my pain out on other people. Before guns got involved, I used to take pellet guns and randomly shoot out the windows of my house or friends' houses and shoot at innocent bystanders. It didn't matter who it was.

I used to treat women bad too. I was so unfair to them. From the age of 15 to about age 22, I used to hang out a lot on 14th Street in southeast DC and run prostitutes to men who were willing to pay these women for sexual favors. Most of the prostitutes were a lot older than me. I would threaten them, and treat them bad by having them sell their bodies, and I didn't give them what they wanted: money. They rightfully earned it, but I was being spiteful and didn't give it to them.

When I was selling crack cocaine, I sold to anyone who wanted a it, including pregnant women, and it didn't even matter to me what I was doing to myself or anyone else.

I used to get so far gone off drugs that I didn't want to live anymore. I thought ending my life was better than the life I was living. I never had anyone tell me "Hey, I'm proud of you."

It wasn't until I was in my 30s, long after my mother had passed, that my cousins told me, "You know, your mom would be real proud of you because she used to pray for you all the time."

I never got that as a young boy trying to figure all this stuff out on my own. Instead those same cousins would put me in a dark room because I was so bad, and leave me in there, and say "You're the devil's kid. You scared?"

My family loved calling me retarded and crazy, but I wasn't retarded. My older brother and I were arguing one day and he stabbed me, right in the heart with a steak knife. Yet they called *me* crazy.

I really had a good heart, I really did. I was just trying to get back at all those people who called me crazy. They said I had the demon in me. But the truth was, I had low self-worth, lies of who I really was, and fear in me; those were my demons within.

Then Jesus demanded, "What is your name?"
And he replied, "My name is Legion, because
there are many of us inside this man."
Mark 5:9 NLT

I thank the Lord for setting me free and He can do the
same for you.

But Jesus said, "No, go home to your family,
and tell them everything the Lord has done for you
and how merciful he has been."
Mark 5:19 NLT

When I was in my late 20s, I moved to Maryland. I used to
go home, by this time I was living by myself, and I would
party all night and wake up the next day in a suit and tie
with vomit all over me and didn't know what happened or
how I ended up where I was. I would leave pans on the
stove that should have set my house on fire, and I'd wake
up the next day and I everything was still the same,
nothing burned. That's the mercy of God.

Years later when my mother passed away the first thing I
wanted to do was go find my dad. I tried to locate him by
asking my family members and other people who might
know him. They told me the little that they knew at the
time, but all it led to was a dead end. I had so much hatred
that I said if I ever do find him, I'm going to kill him.

Fortunately, I never met him. Maybe it was for the best, I
had not yet released that deep-rooted anger and feeling of
abandonment. All those years, having all that hatred in me
for him, had led me to hating everybody.

When I got saved, it became clear. The Lord took me to
Mark 5 and he gave me the story about the demon-
possessed man, and he said, "That was you, but now you're
in your right mind."

So, I got the Lord telling me that the demons had me, that's
why I did the things that I did; but they don't anymore.

GOD DOESN'T MAKE MISTAKES, BUT IF I COULD CHANGE ANYTHING...

When I got saved, I went back to some people who were still alive that I knew and I apologized to them for everything that I did or said and how I treated them. I let them know if I had to change anything, I wouldn't have done it. That's it. If I could reach into the past, the people that I didn't have a chance to say I am sorry to would have that opportunity to hear me say that I am sorry.

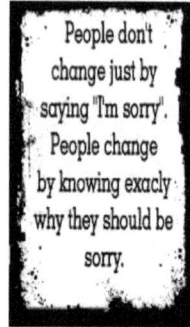

People don't change just by saying "I'm sorry". People change by knowing exactly why they should be sorry.

| *Words of Inspiration and Hope* |

Often times we forget to love on a child who is "different" or we see them as not normal. This child is human. He has feelings, he loves, he likes tenderness and affection just like a child who gets straight-As in school and doesn't have any behavior issues.

Embracing Your Beautiful, Imperfect Child

The internal damage that is done to a child who is abandoned by their father is heart-wrenching. His absence leaves lifelong effects that must be addressed and dealt with head on. It starts with the truth. Be honest with your kids. They need to know the truth. Don't hide anything from them because they will despise you. Let the truth set your child free.

Bullying is also a dangerous game. We lose countless children across America due to children feeling less adequate, unworthy, and afraid to even face those who oppress them. Listen for the signs. Speak to your children often. Know what's going on in their lives, at school, who did what, how did this happen. Build a relationship so your kids will feel comfortable coming to you when they feel any feelings of suicide or unfairness amongst their peers. Children picking on each other is not something to pass off as just kids being kids. It's serious.

Don't ignore any warning signs of your child being on drugs. The first time you suspect something, take them to be tested. You don't want to wait until it's too late. If you find there is some drug use, spend more time with them so you can get to the root of the problem. Many kids just seek attention and are crying out for help.

It is us who builds and shapes our children. We lay the foundation of love, support, encouragement and how they treat people. Be the example you wish your child to be.

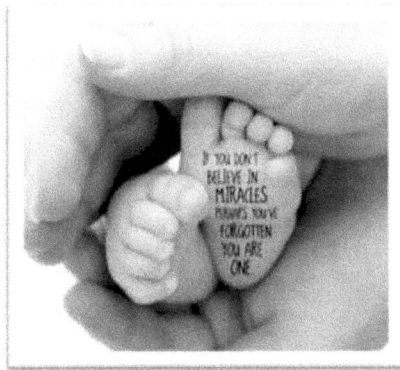

CHAPTER TWO

Running for My Life

THE SECRET SOLACE OF POETRY

When I was a teenager, God's divine direction led me to recite religious poems that I wouldn't tell anyone about. I would sit in my room or walk around reciting poems to myself without even knowing where they came from. I was bad as the devil, but God always reminded me to write down religious poems that talked about Heaven. I used to hide them from everyone; I didn't want anyone to see them because I was seen as this bad guy. I didn't want to ruin my reputation reciting poems.

The Lord's Nature and People

The Lord created nature.

Nature is trees and things around.

But nature you can't see.

You can't see the Lord like you can see the ground.

But you know he's there because nature's there.

He also created people, but some people don't even care.

When the Lord created people, he gave them knowledge to do things.

Knowledge is good, but when you use it wrong,

Like thinking you're on top like a king.

WAS I RUNNING FOR OR RUNNING FROM MY LIFE

The time finally came when I needed to run. I believe that if I would have stayed in that environment, I would have gotten killed, or I would have ended up in jail—one or the other because you don't get out for the sake of getting out. You just don't do that.

When I told my girlfriend it was time to move to Fredericksburg, Virginia, I think I was running from my life. She was from Fredericksburg and I really liked it because it was incredibly peaceful. I was looking to be saved from something so I ran to Virginia, and we ended up staying, around the time I was 33 years old. Within two months I got saved. That's when I ran into the hands of Jesus. That day, I completely changed. I mean, completely. It's really ironic, because I used to joke and laugh at people when they used to talk about Jesus making a difference in their lives and how God had saved them. I used to think they were crazy, but when it happened to me, I said, "Wow! He is real, he is truly real."

GOD THE FATHER REALLY DREW ME TO JESUS

For no one can come to me unless the Father who sent me draws them to me, and at the last day I will raise them up

John 6:44 NLT

I couldn't stop talking about Him. I mean, every day I got into the Word, I just engulfed myself in the Word. I engulfed myself so much people thought I was crazy. They would say I was a Jesus fanatic.

I went from being crazy in the world to being crazy for Jesus. He started really speaking to me about my business, about my calling to pastoring. It was so much and he was telling me things way too fast, so I started to divert back because it was a lot to take in. I started smoking drugs and drinking alcohol, but I was still His.

He said to me, "You're mine, you can't get away now."

I started going back to the naked bars up in DC, even though I felt out of place. I was so confused not really knowing what to do with the guidance I was given.

One evening, the Lord spoke to me while I was in the naked bar, and he said, "What are you doing here?"

I cried for forty-five minutes, all the way home from DC to Fredericksburg. I said, "Lord, I'm sorry."

He had his hand on me so hard. I remember it like it was yesterday. It was powerful. I felt the Lord's heavy presence. It was unreal.

What's crazy is that I always felt this same heavy presence in my life even while I was in the world doing terrible things to people. I always had this thought in my head that it was time to get out and do better for myself. I saw many signs. I didn't know that I was predestined.

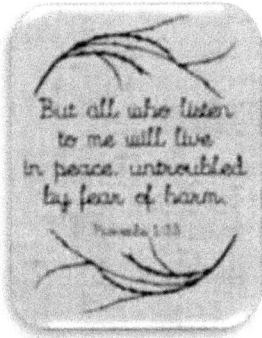

But all who listen to me will live in peace, untroubled by fear of harm.

Proverbs 1:33

I knew you before I formed you in your mother's womb.
Before you were born I set you apart and appointed you as my prophet to the nations.
Jeremiah 1:5 NLT

I was selling drugs real heavy in my early twenties before I moved to Virginia. I used to see police cars that I always felt were following me, as well as other cars driving by that I didn't know. I don't think I was paranoid, but my twelve Rottweilers would do this strange bark and I would go outside. I had an eerie feeling, something didn't seem right. Those incidents led me to be suspicious because some people who I was in the drug game with knew exactly where I lived. I felt like someone was creeping around my house and my dogs were giving me a sign that I know now came from God.

Another sign that told me it was time to change my ways was when I was working in the union. Some of the guys who worked there, who knew what I was up to, were trying to set me up and turn me into the authorities. I think they were informers. I thought, *Either I'm going to get killed or I'm going to go to jail by someone setting me up.* I knew too many things were happening too quickly and I had to get out. The Lord was drawing me to Him.

My wife, of course, always wanted me to get out, but I would give her money, treat her to nice places, and do special things for her that required spending a large amount of money, and that would please her for a little while. My sisters and brothers and some friends also wanted better for me, but it didn't stop them from partaking in the liquor I would bring and the parties I would throw. Therefore, I never took anyone seriously. However, I had my own feelings that I had to get out of the drug game.

What kept me going so long was that in my mind, I thought that I *couldn't* get out. The only way I thought that I could get out was either by death or in jail. I felt if I just stopped all the bad things I was doing, the people I worked for and with would kill me in fear that I would turn them in. In my mind, that's how it was. Once you're in, they don't let you out. You feel this way because you know everything. I mean, you know *everything*. You don't just get out because you decide to. You just don't.

I didn't get too far into the drug scene until after my mother died. Every time she went in the hospital I'd tell the Lord, "I'm going to change my life. I'm going to do better."

At the time, I believed that he said, "Just forget it, I don't believe you."

One day I went in the hospital and she died that very night. I lost it. I threw my fist into the wall of the hospital room. I went outside and I cussed Jesus, I cussed him real bad. This is the time when I said enough is enough. From that point on, I just went really extreme into the world, and got into a lot of things that could have killed me, yet I still didn't care. She died when she was 55; I was 24 years old.

I got deeper into the drug scene by meeting this young man I had a real job with. He was a dealer and I started doing some work for him. Instead of paying me by check, I would sell drugs for him and I made triple the amount of money he was paying me. Naturally, I went for it and from that point on that was it. I was all in. Of course it wasn't long before I quit that job.

Eventually I ran into the hands of Jesus, it was like a relief, a burden came off of me. I didn't have any worries and I no longer cared about what people thought about me. I was willing to tell my testimony about how He was always there with me since day one. It was a great relief. I felt this heavy burden being released from me. The things I used to worry about—my dad and all that—it came off of me. A lot of things came off of me.

Then Jesus said, "Come to me, all of you who are weary and carry heavy burdens, and I will give you rest. Take my yoke upon you. Let me teach you, because I am humble and gentle at heart, and you will find rest for your souls. For my yoke is easy to bear, and the burden I give you is light."
Matthew 11:28-30 NLT

When I got saved, my family members thought I was even crazier and, not surprisingly, they still treated me bad.

Jesus told him, "I am the way, the truth, and the life. No one can come to the Father except through me."
John 14:6 NLT

Some of my family members were supposed to be believers. But once I changed my life over, they would say I was happy, but not *really* happy. They were the main people who used to call me a Jesus fanatic.

One said, "Every time you call me, you don't have to talk about Jesus."

But that's not in the Word. She didn't like talking to me if I talked about Him. If you're a believer, it shouldn't be a problem.

My youngest brother, we never had a relationship, per se. We just tolerated each other. I told him about the change and how new I felt, but it didn't matter to him.

I did a lot of bad things to my family and friends and I pray one day that they will forgive me and truly love me for who I am.

> *But if you refuse to forgive others,*
> *your Father will not forgive your sins*
> **Matthew 6:15 NLT**

My other brother, Charles, it appeared like he didn't believe in the Lord. So he really didn't want to hear what I had to say about Jesus.

They all just called me *more* crazy.

I got in touch with a few of the guys I used to hang with because I was so excited about my new relationship with Jesus and I wanted to tell everyone about Him. They were really happy for me. When I did my first sermon in 2000, a few guys I used to give drugs to came down to witness when I ministered that day. I'll never forget that. When I got married, a few of them came down, and I still keep in touch with some of them now.

When I told others, they didn't want to talk to me anymore, but that is to be expected. I understand now, but back then I didn't get it. I figured everybody would be happy that I changed my life and gave it over to the Lord.

> *If the world hates you, remember that it hated me first. The world would love you as one of its own if you belonged to it, but you are no longer part of the world. I chose you to come out of the world, so it hates you.*
> **John 15:18-19 NLT**

It's so empowering to learn about Jesus and get the Word from God. It's truly life-changing.

This means that anyone who belongs to Christ has become a new person. The old life is gone; a new life has begun!
2 Corinthians 5:17 NLT

Anyone who is searching and doesn't quite know what to do or where to turn, Jesus is the answer.

If you are searching and you don't think Jesus is the answer, first I would ask, "Did you try Him? Did you *truly* try Him?"

I know how it is; in my past life, I tried him a few times. I would have drugs in my suit jacket but just to please my wife I'd say, "Okay, I'm going to give it up and we can go to church." However right after church I would go right back to selling drugs again.

But saying, "I'm giving my life to Him," is a completely different experience, because I have to be honest and ask myself, *Did I really try?* No. No I didn't.

There were times when I tried Jesus to appease other people. I'm not saying that everybody has to reach their bottom in the sense that a tragedy has to happen. But I do believe that we reach a point in our lives where we all are searching for the truth. I do believe that as we live out our journeys in life, if we can look back to some of our encounters where we can't believe how we got out of a mess, we have to believe in our hearts, mind, and soul that that right there was Jesus. Those encounters where you have no clue how you made it through. That's nobody but Jesus.

In that way, you will be acting as true children of your Father in heaven. For he gives his sunlight to both the evil and the good, and he sends rain on the just and the unjust alike.
Matthew 5:45 NLT

You don't always have to get with somebody who knows the Word or who is a pastor. That may not work for everybody. My advice is to lock yourself in a room with just you and Him, and talk to Him like he's right in front of you. Tell him what's on your mind and in your heart, and ask him to lead you from that point on, whether it's in the Word, or you just sitting still. There have been incidents where I opened up the Bible and the words just seemed to jump off the page, and I knew that He was speaking to me. It was real. I believe being alone with Him, and just talking to Him is the best advice I can give you to remove the burdens of your life. Be ready to receive.

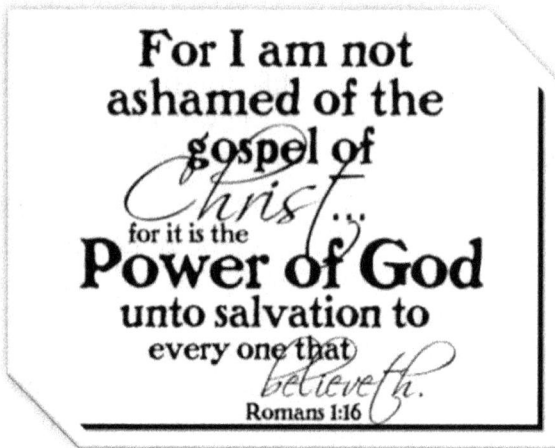

> **For I am not ashamed of the gospel of Christ...** for it is the **Power of God** unto salvation to every one that believeth.
> **Romans 1:16**

He is the Holy Spirit, who leads into all truth. The world cannot receive him, because it isn't looking for him and doesn't recognize him. But you know him, because he lives with you now and later will be in you.
JOHN 14:17 NLT

CHAPTER THREE

Building Houses

I stayed back in school a couple times and also dropped out a few times, but I finally went back to finish my trade certificate in carpentry when I was about 22 years old.

When I eventually moved to the suburbs of Virginia in my 30s, I started to live better but I couldn't get a good job or keep one. I was just so in love with Jesus. All I wanted to do was read the Word, spend time with Him, and go to church. That was my life.

My wife kept saying that I needed to find a job. I would go to the 7-11 and get a newspaper and act like I was looking for a job, and when she would leave, I would spend time with the Lord. Every day I would do this. Sometimes, I would find work, but I would get laid off because I talked about the Lord and didn't spend too much time working.

One day, I was on this job in DC when the FedEx Field was being built. What the Lord showed me that day was the Scripture in Luke 15:17...

When he finally came to his senses, he said to himself, "At home even the hired servants have food enough to spare, and here I am dying of hunger!"
Luke 15:17 NLT

...and the Lord told me, "I've got better for you."

I was working outside where it was cold and muddy. I had cold metal studs to screw into the beams, and it was just a mess out there.

He said "I've got better for you."

That day, I quit.

I ended up coming home, and you can't tell a black woman you just quit your job. She will not want to hear that. So I never told her that I quit my job.

I just kept seeking the Lord in my prayer room, and he said to me, "Start your own business."

I talked to him plain and out loud. "How can I start a business when I can't even keep a job? I don't know anything about it."

And he said, "I'll show you."

Then, a month or two later, in 1997, Pastor T.D. Jakes was preaching at the MCI Center in D.C., and I heard a good Word from him. Usually when the Lord speaks to me He then confirms it through people.

As I listened to T.D. Jakes, the Lord said, "Remember your name was Big Mack. I want you to remember that some of the people who are here in this building used to be called these street names, too, and were street hustlers just like you were. Now you all are deacons, ministers, and pastors. So listen, you guys were slinging dope but guess what? That takes a business mind."

He said, "The same way that you used to run the dope— you get the stuff, cook it up, cut it up, give it to the runners. You tell them what you expect back. They make a little something on it, they bring back your profit, and you keep doing it over and over again. And you kept on excelling. It's the same thing in business, but your own legit business. All you have to do to start your own company and use that business mind in a positive way and you can succeed."

T.D. Jakes said, "You can make profit by being honest."

When he said that, I started crying because I knew that it was the Lord speaking. It was meant for me to go all the way to DC to hear that message again. God brought it to me again after the time he told me in my prayer room. Start my own business. I thank God for Reverend Crisp taking me to go see Bishop T.D. Jakes. It changed my life.

So I went home that day and I said to the Lord, "Okay, if this is real, you are going to have to show me because I have no idea how to start a business or what to do."

Then, He started directing me to people who were a lot sharper than I was, and they started to point me in right direction.

The Lord gave me the name Trinity Construction Company, Inc.

For every house has a builder,
but the one who built everything is God.
Hebrews 3:4 NLT

I went to brother Rippy who was a good friend of mine, and I told him that the Lord wants me to start my own business and asked him how I go about it.

He told me to go down to the county and fill out the paperwork for Trinity Construction, Inc., and so that's what I did. I started passing out flyers. I told people about my business. This led to small construction work in the church for people. At first I wasn't charging people, but then I began setting pricing for my services and the business grew from there.

I was being authentic and honest with people, like the Lord advised me. It grew to the point where I was able to go all the way up to my B license, which authorized me to build houses. I did a lot of work for people building their homes or doing remodels throughout the Fredericksburg area.

Our company motto was *Build with Us*; we also were building lives.

I went from not knowing what to do, to God saying, "I'll show you," to having 10 employees and three secretaries.

But then I got prideful and the Lord took it from me.

> *Hear and give ear: Do not be proud,*
> *For the LORD has spoken.*
> **Jeremiah 13:15 NKJV**

I had said to the Lord, "When you raise me up this time, I'm never going to forget you. Never."

In T.D. Jakes' audio series, he says in the message, "Okay, when you get to a certain point, don't start buying suits and all that because you know you can do it. Start putting away and start saving."

I heard but I didn't do that. I did the opposite. I started buying cars and buying suits. I had three and four and five cars, just paying cash for them. I was doing a whole lot of reckless stuff, not thinking about my actions at all.

I thought it was all about me. I started putting the business over the Lord. I forgot He was the one who gave it to me. That happens often, and many people are going through that right now. They forget about God, and don't realize it was God who gave them their success, and they get prideful.

> *Remember, you must not make any idols of silver*
> *or gold to rival me.*
> **Exodus 20:23 NLT**

In 2006, the economy started to shift. What it says in the Word...

> *Once I was young, and now I am old. Yet I have never seen*
> *the godly abandoned or their children begging for bread.*
> **Psalm 37:25 NLT**

...therefore I understand that this economy in the world is different from God's economy. But, by me being prideful in where I was and my state of mind, I ended up allowing that to happen. Things got to the point where, as my business was collapsing, I had to do a lot of cutting back. I had to cut back office overhead expenses and move it back to my home. I had to cut my employees, and the contracts weren't coming in like they were coming in before. I couldn't sustain.

Around 2007 is when it really hit my business hard. The housing market plummeted so for a whole year, even if I could afford to I couldn't buy a job. And what I mean by that is, I tried to even work at McDonalds, but nobody was hiring. Everything was shut down, and I was crying out to the Lord.

> *My brethren, count it all joy*
> *when you fall into various trials.*
> **James 1:2 NKJV**

Well, it didn't seem too joyful at the time.

Then my wife got our mortgage lender to approve us for the stimulus package so that we could avoid our home going into foreclosure. The Lord worked everything out after that year.

Let me tell you how God works. Our mortgage got cut in half and our lender put all our past due balances, interest, and fees on the back end of our loan so we started from scratch, and then the Lord blessed me with a job at VSE.

I was blessed with that job for a few years and he told me, "Start giving Me the praise and the honor," and from that point on that's what I did.

*Now the LORD blessed the latter days of Job more than his
beginning; for he had fourteen thousand sheep,
six thousand camels, one thousand yoke of oxen, and one
thousand female donkeys.*

Job 42:12 NKJV

MY GREATEST GIFT THUS FAR IN MY LIFE HAS BEEN MY GIFT TO MINISTER

After I got saved, a woman named Ms. Mary prophesized to me. I was doing an odd job at her home and she told me that the Lord was going to bless me with a business, and I was going to deal with a lot of sick people who really needed me.

She was exactly right.

In 1995, before I was pastoring I was called to minister. I would go in the jail and witness to people. I started my construction business in 1998. We first opened up Trinity Fellowship International Church in 2005.

My construction business was an avenue to be able to witness and not just to people who worked for me, but also to people that I did work for. God was moving through that business.

Once I opened my business, people were coming into my life with all their problems. Some of those included drug addictions and they used to steal from me, but I used to counsel them and try to see the best in them. I had been there and done all that, so I ministered to them because I knew they were not crazy. I know that this was my purpose: to minister.

Even when I was younger, going through the things I was going through, I remember ministering to people in some way or another. It was my calling.

I used to have talks with Him all the time and every time I messed up, I knew He was mad at me.

As I mentioned before I would recite a lot of religious poetry that I had long forgotten when I was older and dealing drugs. When I got saved a lot of those poems came back to me. I used to have a lot of them written down, but there are only two that I remember by heart. It's amazing that God brought them right back to me.

I Have A Dream

I have a dream that
I'll respect all the Ten Commandments before they go dim
I have a dream that if I die before I do my name isn't Tim
I have a dream that someone will say to me Tim who are you
I will say I was a person who was sad and blue
But now I have a dream that is no dream it's realistic
because I will be with Him
It's no longer a dream
because my name is Tim

Once I got saved, it just popped back to me, word for word. At that time, people were calling me crazy, and they thought they were so smart, but they judged me to be less than them. If you don't recognize Him, you aren't anything without Him.

MINISTERING TO PEOPLE: BUILDING LIVES

It's not important who does the planting, or who does the watering. What's important is that God makes the seed grow. The one who plants and the one who waters work together with the same purpose. And both will be rewarded for their own hard work. For we are both God's workers. And you are God's field. You are God's building.
1 Corinthians 3:7-9 NLT

The Lord has shown me that people will come to me and trust themselves with me with whatever they were dealing with. They didn't have to know me either. It wasn't just my workers, but also the customers—white, black, Spanish—it didn't matter. It didn't matter at all.

The Lord spoke me one day and said, "I call you to be a mouthpiece for me."

He sent me into these big houses to talk about Him. That door would be open. It was crazy. Some of the places and homes I was doing work for, I would never have dreamed that I would be talking about the Lord with these strangers, but he put me in that place, and I know it was his plan to see all this and have this beautiful experience, and to say what he wanted me to say, and take it from there.

In the same way, let your good deeds shine out for all to see, so that everyone will praise your heavenly Father.
Matthew 5:16 NLT

There were a few incidents where people would thank me for bringing them closer to the Lord and tell me that I helped bring them out of something they had been dealing with for a very long time.

There were some incidents where I would give them Scriptures to read, or they would ask, "Where can I find this information?"

They wanted to go deeper. They would say that they had been searching for this for a while. "Wow, you finally hit it on the head." Things like that they would let me know. Sometimes, they wouldn't let me know, but you got that sense. Like you know that you hit something. Like the Holy Ghost would just be in the place, you'd just know. It's not you that hit it, but it's Him, and you were just there to speak His words.

The Lord was speaking through me to change people's lives.

| **Words of Inspiration and Hope** |

Pastor Wormley used to always tell me to pass it on. He was always giving to me of his time and I always thanked him. So I follow his advice and just pass it on.

We must stay humble and remember where we came from. Always look back on your past, not in a shameful way, but just see how far God has brought you. I do believe when you keep that type of perspective, it just helps you. Continue to do what you were doing before you got to the point of where you're at now—that's in the Word. I realize when I started vacationing I lost focus. The word is just to stay humble. When people pat you on the back and praise you, just say, "Hey, that's God."

CHAPTER FOUR

From Pushing Dope to Pushing Hope

Oh, how generous and gracious our Lord was!
He filled me with the faith and love that come from Christ
Jesus.
This is a trustworthy saying, and everyone should accept it:
"Christ Jesus came into the world to save sinners" and I am
the worst of them all. But God had mercy on me so that Christ
Jesus could use me as a prime example of his great patience
with even the worst sinners. Then others will realize that
they, too, can believe in him and receive eternal life. All honor
and glory to God forever and ever! He is the eternal King, the
unseen one who never dies; he alone is God. Amen.
1 Timothy 1:14-17 NLT

HOW CAN I HELP SOMEONE GET THROUGH A TOUGH SITUATION?

The Book of Psalms talks about if the house is not built by the Lord, they labor in vain. It lets us know that we all are building an edifice, the body of Christ. We must refrain from negative criticism if we wish to do God's work of service.

27

Unless the LORD builds the house, They labor in vain who build it; Unless the LORD guards the city, The watchman stays awake in vain.

Psalm 127:1 NKJV

If the foot should say, "Because I am not a hand, I am not of the body," is it therefore not of the body?
And if the ear should say, "Because I am not an eye, I am not of the body," is it therefore not of the body?
If the whole body were an eye, where would be the hearing? If the whole were hearing, where would be the smelling?
But now God has set the members, each one of them, in the body just as He pleased.

1 Corinthians 12:15-18 NKJV

We all have to work together in life without discrimination or looking down on people or belittling them—none of that. We are to be about lifting them up and building them up. Life and death are in the power of the tongue, so it's important for us to speak life. Let's speak on what we might not see with our eyes but what we know in our hearts someone has the potential to become. If you keep speaking life to someone, they are going to believe it for themselves, and it will come to pass. Speaking life gives someone validation and encouragement.

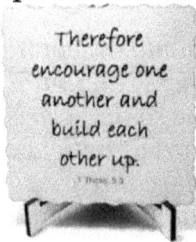

Therefore encourage one another and build each other up.
1 Thess. 5:3

God, who gives life to the dead and calls those things which do not exist as though they did.

Romans 4:17 NKJV

WHY IS IT IMPORTANT TO SHARE YOUR TESTIMONY?

So never be ashamed to tell others about our Lord. And don't be ashamed of me, either, even though I'm in prison for him. With the strength God gives you, be ready to suffer with me for the sake of the Good News.

2 Timothy 1:8 NLT

I know all about that feeling there. When you are able to share your life experiences a lot of burden will be lifted off of you. It is very scary for me to share my experiences with you, and also extremely painful, but what I've learned is that it is also necessary for balance in my life. It is therapeutic as well and in the process of sharing, my burdens have been lifted.

Sharing your story is not just for *you*; it serves as an opportunity to help someone else that is going through, been through, or coming to what you have already experienced. You're able to help someone else, and that's the other part to building somebody up. You give them hope, helping them to believe in themselves and believe in the God that created them and that they can do all things through Christ Jesus who strengthens them.

That is so important. Once you get it out, you just feel so much better and so strengthened. It's really all about passing it on and helping somebody else.

WHAT IF I DON'T HAVE ANYONE TO SUPPORT ME?

*Jesus asked, "Do you finally believe? But the time is coming-
indeed it's here now-when you will be scattered,
each one going his own way, leaving me alone.
Yet I am not alone because the Father is with me.
I have told you all this so that you may have peace in me.
Here on earth you will have many trials and sorrows.
But take heart, because I have overcome the world.*
John 16:31-33 NLT

*Dear brothers and sisters, when troubles of any kind come
your way, consider it an opportunity for great joy.
For you know that when your faith is tested,
your endurance has a chance to grow. So let it grow,
for when your endurance is fully developed,
you will be perfect and complete, needing nothing.*
James 1:2-4 NLT

I've been there so I get it. Try to stay focused even though it's difficult. I believe without a doubt that the challenges that come in life, and the challenges we put on ourselves are eventually going to turn around.

Success is owning up to your choices. It is being the driving force in your own life with no excuses.

It's going to be a collaboration of things that are going to strengthen you and not hurt you. Your trials are there to help you go further in life. Therefore, that is something that is important to share. Even though all of these things happened to me and I made so many terrible decisions, in the end it actually strengthened me to help others.

I'M STRUGGLING TO BE A GOOD MAN. WHAT IS YOUR ADVICE?

Without wise leadership, a nation falls;
there is safety in having many advisers.
Proverbs 11:14 NLT

When I was growing up my mother used to tell me to try to hang with someone who is more successful than me. Spend your time around people who are better than you in the sense that they have something positive on their minds like goals and strong ethics and they are going somewhere. Eventually, that positivity will be an inspiration and will end up rubbing off on you.

PEOPLE DON'T CHANGE. THEIR PRIORITES DO.

It's really a mindset shift, and it will end up changing your mind from the way you used to think, and make you want to do better. If you hang around thugs and gangsters, and never ask more of yourself, then that's what you are going to become. But if you hang around positive people who are focused on going somewhere successfully, then that's what you are going to become. You are who you hang with so choose wisely.

I'M A WOMAN AND PEOPLE TRY TO STOP ME FROM LIVING RIGHT. HOW DO I GET PAST IT?

Don't copy the behavior and customs of this world, but let God transform you into a new person by changing the way you think. Then you will learn to know God's will for you, which is good and pleasing and perfect.
Romans 12:2 NLT

Let this mind be in you, which was also in Christ Jesus.
Philippians 2:5 KJV

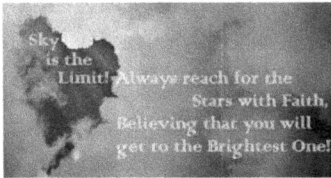

I have noticed just through my past experiences that you're not crazy no matter what people may think of you or how they try to identify you. Their opinions of you do not matter. God gives us great minds to go beyond what we could ever imagine or dream of accomplishing. There's an old saying that says the stars are the limit and I really believe that with his help and His direction, you can accomplish anything, overcome any adversity in your life—anything.

STRUGGLING WITH PAIN OF LEAVING MY CHILDREN

One day the widow of a member of the group of prophets came to Elisha and cried out, "My husband who served you is dead, and you know how he feared the LORD. But now a creditor has come, threatening to take my two sons as slaves."
"What can I do to help you?" Elisha asked. "Tell me, what do you have in the house?"
"Nothing at all, except a flask of olive oil," she replied.
And Elisha said, "Borrow as many empty jars as you can from your friends and neighbors. Then go into your house with your sons and shut the door behind you. Pour olive oil from your flask into the jars, setting each one aside when it is filled."

So she did as she was told. Her sons kept bringing jars to her, and she filled one after another. Soon every container was full to the brim!
"Bring me another jar," she said to one of her sons.
"There aren't any more!" he told her. And then the olive oil stopped flowing.
When she told the man of God what had happened, he said to her, "Now sell the olive oil and pay your debts, and you and your sons can live on what is left over."

2 Kings 4:1-7 NLT

If you have any open opportunity, if there is still time left, then you can still make it right. Don't allow yourself or your children to leave this earth without trying to get it right despite what may have transpired. Whether it's your fault, or the other person's fault, you can still make it right.

Remember, it's not the child's fault so he or she doesn't deserve to miss out on a relationship with you over a disagreement or selfishness. Think about that child first and try your best to make it right despite how you may feel—the pride, the hurt, the way things happened. Just try to get it right with your kids.

It's important so that your child will know the truth. He doesn't have to go in his grave without knowing his father

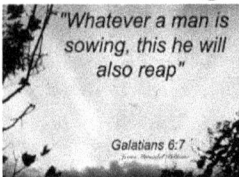
"Whatever a man is sowing, this he will also reap"
Galatians 6:7

or mother. He won't have to assume things and create his own story. When you don't know you assume. And that's one thing you don't want, for a kid to assume. Usually they assume the worst and decide in their young minds to take the blame for everything. This blame can lead to suicide. It's really that serious nowadays with the pressures these kids have in the world. So consider the emotions of that child. They need you.

My Father Left Me. What Can I Do?

*One God and Father of all, who is above all,
and through all, and in you all.*
Ephesians 4:6 KJV

Try your best to forgive your dad, number one. Try to search for him as there's nothing wrong with trying to find him. Do everything in your power to try to find him and forgive him. With forgiveness, you are able to move on with life. Without forgiving, you cannot move on because the past will always haunt you. When you forgive you are able to move on and you are able to be aware of what is going on without having bitterness in your heart.

When you live in bitterness, you are not able to love people the way God wants you to love them and you aren't able to respect them the way God wants you to. Of course, the pain may still be there. It's like a wound. When the Band-Aid comes off the reminder is still there. There's nothing wrong with that, but you have to forgive.

Whatever you may have already gone through—whatever challenges, whatever obstacles have already come your way or are coming your way, whatever the world tries to put on you. Even the enemy—the devil, he's real, the demons, they're real—whatever they try to do to block your destination, know that you can triumph through it all with the help of the Lord Jesus.

Every problem is an opportunity to trust God

CHAPTER FIVE

They Say You're Crazy

People will try to talk about you as if you are the devil's child yourself. Don't let this stop you. You are *not* crazy!

People who lack love, self-confidence, and self-respect will unconsciously try to make you feel that whatever you are doing is not right because they do not have the confidence and courage to do it for themselves. They will try to make you think you are not worthy of God's promise and try to push you from your purpose. You are not crazy. Keep up the fight and let those people know you are not finished yet.

It's so important to not let your past dictate your future. Just because you have done things you may not be proud of, that does not mean your life is over and that you must stay in the past. Remember that your past serves as lessons. Take a look at the lesson, learn from it and move on. Pray and seek God's advice and take positive steps in the right direction. God has a plan for your life. You do not want to disappoint Him because He is the one who gave you the struggle to test your faith in Him. Overcome and fight for your life. Your past does not define you. You are not crazy!

Love yourself enough to do what's right for you and your life. You do not have to please anyone. Your life is yours to live and you are the only one responsible for your happiness. Once you find the Lord and know the Lord you will seek his love and receive his favor. You have nothing to worry about as God's got your back. Often times we fear the unknown. We don't know what's next so we don't take that next necessary step that could move us forward.

Instead we live in our fear, in comfort, and never overcome our limits. I want you to get comfortable being uncomfortable. Know that everything you want in your life is outside of your comfort zone.

For God has not given us a spirit of fear
and timidity,
but of power, love, and self-discipline.
2 Timothy 1:7 NLT

Think of the comfort zone as this bubble. Inside that bubble is contentment, pain, lack, limitations, fear, and negativity. Now look at that same bubble and see yourself breaking through it. What do you see? See happiness, possibility, no limitations, positive change, and success.

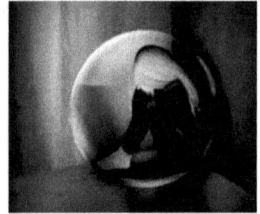

The things we want for ourselves do not live in that comfort bubble. Everything is outside of that. Reach for it. Touch it. Grab it real tight and remove every fear and limitation you have. It's not fair to God to hold yourself in fear. He does not want that for you. He put you here on Earth for a purpose. Don't disappoint him. You are not crazy!

Stay true to who God created you to be. This is your truth. He made none of us crazy. He doesn't even work that way. He made you whole and with purpose. Ask Him what He has put you here to do and listen to what He brings you. Don't go against it. Trust me. You are not crazy.

I will praise thee; for I am fearfully and wonderfully made:
marvelous are thy works; and that
my soul knoweth right well.
Psalm 139:14 KJV

People called me a Jesus fanatic and hated to see me coming. But God told me to go spread His word so that I could heal His people and bring them closer to Him. I didn't care that they called me crazy. I knew I had a purpose so I listened to my spirit. The spirit doesn't lie. We only lie to ourselves when we place limitations on ourselves.

Many people thought I wouldn't amount to anything. But God had another plan. I'm not crazy. You're not crazy.

Seek God and knowledge, and whatever you are called to do, do it fearlessly, courageously as God would want you to do. Don't let anything or anyone stop you. The only person who can hold you back is you.

You intended to harm me, but God intended it all for good. He brought me to this position so I could save the lives of many people.
Genesis 50:20 NLT

Yes, I had some issues in my past that I could have let prevent me from the life I have now. Yes, I would just go up to a stranger and start some fights with them and go into the stores and walk out with stuff I didn't pay for. I didn't care at that time. But God had a plan for me, and I didn't make up an excuse not to listen. I wanted better, so I listened to God and let him guide me.

You're not crazy.

CHAPTER SIX

Ministry and Restoration

TRINITY FELLOWSHIP INTERNATIONAL CHURCH

We started our church in 2005 at Houston's Night Club in Fredericksburg. We opened the doors and the first service was September 11 at eight o'clock that morning. We had a great service. My Pastor Wormley was there.

We started our small church with just 12 people who were willing to come along with us. However, there were over 100 people in attendance at the first service. Relatives came from all over to celebrate and witness what God was doing.

We eventually moved to our own building where we've been since 2007.

We believe in the Lord and this church will be a resource center for the community in the coming years, and we are going to meet their needs.

And though you started with little, you will end with much.
Job 8:7 NLT

Right now, we are set up to feed people, anyone that is in need, about once a week. We can clothe them from our clothing ministry and we are setting up our computer lab. We believe in the Lord that people are going to come and look for jobs on the Internet and learn computer and leadership skills. We believe that the Lord is going to set us up with grants to fund what we're trying to do. We just want to be a help to the community, and also be there to help people that transition out of jail. We believe in the Lord that we will have a building where they can come and find housing, and not just housing, but be able to get some type of spiritual guidance to change their behavior, to change their ways, and to change their lives. We also believe in the Lord that we will be a place of shelter for those who need it because there are only a few shelters in the area currently.

There are people who need extended help so we want to be able to provide that for them as well. I have been through that before—homeless and hungry—so I want to lend a helping hand.

The Final Judgment
But when the Son of Man comes in his glory, and all the angels with him, then he will sit upon his glorious throne. All the nations will be gathered in his presence, and he will separate the people as a shepherd separates the sheep from the goats. He will place the sheep at his right hand and the goats at his left.
Then the King will say to those on his right," Come, you who are blessed by my Father, inherit the Kingdom prepared for you from the creation of the world. For I was hungry, and you fed me. I was thirsty,
and you gave me a drink. I was a stranger, and you invited me into your home. I was naked, and you gave me clothing. I was sick, and you cared for me. I was in prison, and you visited me."
Matthew 25:31-36 NLT

We just want to be the type of people that we were called to be and that is to help people. We want to be a help in the community or wherever God sends our way. We will do His work.

God gave me the vision to plant churches throughout the state in various communities. Through God's will we have been able to plant a church in Maryland where I lived. The mission is *restoration*. Restoring back to God, and then restoring each other. The Lord showed me that before we started; because He always tells me while we're doing the thing or before I do it...He showed me that it's not just about my family, but other families up there that I had a relationship with. I want them back, I want a relationship. He's the pursuer, and he wants to restore the families.

And then in the midst of all this is the restoration to each other, where they love each other and really care for each other. So far, seeing the majority of the people there, that's the type of people they are; they are mending their relationships with the Lord and then to each other.

The Lord also showed me that we will be opening up another church in Fredericksburg and we have a pastor in place to run that church. They have faithful members already in their leadership, and the Lord is going to free me up real soon where I am going to be able to travel. And when I say churches, I'm not building just to have someone there, but really have the heart of God present because that is so important to have the heart of God. Jeremiah 3:15 talks about, *I will send you shepherds after my own heart.* The churches that the Lord is asking me to open will have the heart of God.

"My heart is fixed. O God, my heart is fixed on You: I will sing; yes, I will sing praises." Psalm 57:7

BODY RESTORATION

When I am caught up in the ministry, the spirit fills me. I find it is easier to focus my attention on giving to others, and it is less appealing for me to be attentive to my own health. Recognizing this imbalance has been a hard lesson for me to learn.

But I discipline my body and keep it under control, lest after preaching to others I myself should be disqualified.
1 Corinthians 9:27

I admit that I have some health problems, and that I've had these conditions for a very long time. Even though I have tried to eat healthy foods I'm overweight, and the Lord has been dealing with me on that for a long time. The doctors said I have diabetes, high blood pressure, sarcoidosis, asthma—you name it, and I've probably got it.

Do you not know that you are God's temple
and that God's Spirit dwells in you?
If anyone destroys God's temple, God will destroy him.
For God's temple is holy, and you are that temple.
1 Corinthians 3:16-17

I remember going to the heart doctor for the first time. It was my first time ever meeting Dr. Askait and his nurse Ms. Tia. I was in his office, and he was checking me over.

"I see your list of medicines here," he said and asked me questions on a few of them.

I said, "I know I can get off these medicines, but it's hard."

I told him that I can pray for people healing, lay hands on them, and I can see them get healed, but when it comes to myself—I started crying—I can't lay hands on myself, nothing can happen. This fat struggle has been my downfall and it's going to kill me. I don't want to die.

So, he said to me, "Do you want to change?"

"Yes, I do."

"This is your day. I'm going to bring in an assistant nurse, and she is going to pray for you."

She came in and she prayed—I never met her until that day and yet she prayed for me. I found out they were both believers in Christ.

He said, "I believe on this day, you're going to change."

42

I said, "You know what, I believe it too."

I remember that Sunday going to church, I preached a sermon. In that sermon, I talked about some things that the Lord does for us, and the Lord spoke to me as I was talking about what happened in that doctor's office.

He said, "There's a part that you play."

I told the congregation that the Lord just said there's a part that you play. He can put these tools out there. He can put this healthy eating here or this exercise there. But there's a part that *we* play. What he's telling me and telling us is that we have to take part of this. We have to want it. We have to control and discipline ourselves. From that point on, I saw changes. A lot of people didn't believe me, even my wife didn't believe it, but I listened to God and I have already lost over 30 pounds.

I went to take my A1C blood sugar; it went from 76 to 6.8. I'm believing in the Lord when I go back next time it's going to be down to six and then it's going to go down from that. I just believe in the Lord that he intervened on that day—that it was a God encounter. I am honoring God's presence in my life with my choice to continue the work He has begun in restoring my body.

I tried everything, and I was never able to lose the weight and feel good. My wife will tell you it got to the point where I couldn't even carry a case of water in the house up the steps. Now, I can carry it over my shoulder without breathing hard because I've been exercising too, which plays a huge part on my energy and overall health.

The Lord used that doctor and that nurse who were there for me. Their ministry is healing the physical body. Since then, she and I have met a couple of times to discuss healthy eating and how to change my lifestyle. I've pretty much got things down now. I thank God for her. She's even willing to come to the church and do a class free of charge to just talk about health—because the Lord will always put you in the presence of people who have been-there, done-that.

She told me her testimony and, like me, she also took a lot of medicine. She got off all her medicine, not on a blood pressure pill, not on diabetic medicine or any of that.

The Lord told her, "I want you to be around because you have work to do," so she started listening to Him. She wrote up what she could about healthy eating. From John 15:1 the name of her business is True Vine. I thank the Lord for that encounter, and the opportunity to share.

> *For I can do everything through Christ,*
> *who gives me strength.*
> **Philippians 4:13 NLT**

You just have to want it bad enough as you claim you do. Sometimes God has to speak to us. You have to listen and take the necessary action to transform your life.

> *But be doers of the word,*
> *and not hearers only, deceiving yourselves.*
> **James 1:22 NKJV**

CHAPTER SEVEN

He Called Me to Preach

I got saved in 1995. The Lord was dealing with me early on. It seemed like I couldn't even step on a bug, he was so hard on me. I always felt like other people could get away with stuff, but not me. I didn't know at the time what he was doing. He was just purifying me is what I know now. He was getting me ready for ministry, but at the time I didn't know.

So, one day I had a talk with the Lord, and I asked him why was he so hard on me. He took me to the Book of Hebrews.

No discipline is enjoyable while it is happening-it's painful! But afterward there will be a peaceful harvest of right living for those who are trained in this way.
Hebrews 12:11 NLT

When I read that, I started crying and I told him, "You must really love me because you chastise me all the time." I vowed to always stay in the Word, to always spend time with Him.

One night, I was home by myself and I was in the scriptures, it was as if the Lord was right next to me, He spoke so clearly. He talked to me about preaching. I thought I was losing my mind because after hearing my sister and a few other people say I'm a Jesus fanatic—I even had people in the church telling me they needed to take me bowling or to the movies or something because I'm in it too deep.

I started having my past hit me and I started questioning myself, "Maybe I *am* crazy. Maybe I am taking it too far."

But when the Lord spoke to me about preaching I *really* thought I was losing my mind. My wife didn't understand me. Nobody understood what I was going through. So, when He spoke that to me, I said to Him, "I can't do it. I just can't do it. I don't know how to do it."

Then, he took me to Exodus...

> *But Moses pleaded with the LORD, "O Lord, I'm not very good with words. I never have been, and I'm not now, even though you have spoken to me. I get tongue-tied, and my words get tangled."*
> *Then the LORD asked Moses, "Who makes a person's mouth? Who decides whether people speak or do not speak, hear or do not hear, see or do not see? Is it not I, the LORD? Now go! I will be with you as you speak, and I will instruct you in what to say."*
> *But Moses again pleaded, "Lord, please! Send anyone else."*
> **Exodus 4:10-13 NLT**

He took me to that, and He kept saying in the Scripture, "Who made your tongue? Who gave you the mouth?"

After that, I shut the Bible, and I cut off every light in the house, and I just sat there crying out to Him. It was too much for me. That's when I started to revert back to my old ways.

I got some connections up the road, and I started getting high. I just thought I was really gone. Maybe they were right. Maybe I was in too deep. So, as I was doing that, I was still hearing the Lord's voice telling me that I'm His, and I can't get away from Him now.

"It's too late; you're mine."

> *And I will ask the Father, and he will give you another Advocate, who will never leave you. He is the Holy Spirit, who leads into all truth. The world cannot receive him, because it isn't looking for him and doesn't recognize him. But you know him, because he lives with you now and later will be in you.*
> **John 14:16-17 NLT**

I said before that I went up to DC and went to the naked bar and it didn't feel right, and the Lord said, "What are you doing there?" And I just left.

So some weeks went by, and then I finally said to the Lord, "Okay, if this is really you"—because every so often I'd ask him that—"you've got to prove it to me. You've got to tell me, you've got to do something."

He told me to go and see my pastor. I met with my pastor four or five times, and each time that we met, I never told him what I was really there for. I just made up other stuff and was talking to him.

The last time when I met with him, I said, "I come to you all the time and I really haven't told you what I'm really supposed to tell you."

He said, "What is that?"

I told him, "Drinking wine and everything—I think I'm really losing it. The Lord is telling me that he wants me to preach. He assured me when I go in the jail—He said, 'Feed my sheep. Do you love me?' And I said, 'Yeah.' And he said, 'Feed my sheep.' And then he showed me that's what I'm doing now."

After breakfast Jesus asked Simon Peter, "Simon son of John, do you love me more than these?"
"Yes, Lord," Peter replied, "you know I love you."
"Then feed my lambs," Jesus told him. Jesus repeated the question: "Simon son of John, do you love me?"
"Yes, Lord," Peter said, "You know I love you."
"Then take care of my sheep," Jesus said. A third time he asked him, "Simon son of John, do you love me?"
Peter was hurt that Jesus asked the question a third time. He said, "Lord, you know everything. You know that I love you."
Jesus said, "Then feed my sheep."
John 21:15-17 NLT

He said, "You're doing it now. They tell you everything, and you don't judge them, you don't look down on them. You're being a shepherd now to my people."

When I shared that with my pastor, I told him, "I don't know what to do."

Then he started laughing at me, and I said, "Why are you laughing at me?"

"The mark is on you. We've seen it for a long time."

"Why didn't you say something to me?"

"I couldn't. I had to let the Lord work that out in you."

We set up a few more meetings after that to talk about the calling. He helped me out tremendously. We set up a date to do my initial sermon, and it was called—I remember it really well—"Cover or Not, He Sees You Just as You Are." We cannot hide from Him.

That's how I started preaching. I was called by God. I ran from it for a couple of years, I ran from Him. I wanted no part of this at all. I'm sure at the time my wife didn't want it either. This calling demanded that we refocus our lives.

We weren't married just yet and we would argue all the time. The life that I wanted to live was completely opposite of the life she was used to. It was a rough stage in our relationship.

I was attending Pastor Tillman's church and he was preaching because they didn't have a pastor at the time. When you go to a church for the first time, sometimes they say visitors stand up. When we stood, all eyes were on us, and I felt uncomfortable so I introduced Cheri as my wife and said these are our kids.

I had no idea God was going to speak to me that day. We went home and I said, "Honey, we've got to go back to that church. We've got to tell him the truth that we're not married."

We agreed and told him and he said, "Y'all planning on getting married?"

We said, "Yeah," and in time we got married. The church helped plan everything for us. They showed us so much love.

After that, it was pure hell. That's the only way I can say it, pure hell. My wife and I would party hard. We'd take a half gallon of Tanqueray gin, and it would be gone in one night and it was only just me and her, knocked out cold. That's how we lived—just living for the moment.

When I got saved, some things changed immediately. It's like a light bulb turned on and my thinking was clear. It was as if the Lord took out my eyes and put His eyes in. I saw people positively and I saw life plain as day. These changes started to happen, and my speech changed. I went from cussing and thug talking to no cussing, no talking dirty, none of that. I was in church almost every day from that point on.

For you have been born again,
but not to a life that will quickly end.
Your new life will last forever because it comes from
the eternal, living word of God.
1 Peter 1:23 NLT

My wife and I used to party sometimes during the week and Saturdays but there could be no more of that.

It got to the point where she would say, "Come on, let's do something."

I would say okay, but as I was doing what she wanted, the Lord would speak to me. He was convicting me. I remember waking up one day, and I just cried out to Him. I told Him, "I'm sorry, I'm sorry."

My wife said, "What's wrong with you?"

I told her God isn't happy with me. He's not happy with what I'm doing.

Every time I called her, I would want to share about Jesus and she didn't want to hear it. In person, she didn't want to hear it either. So she would go down to her mom or pop's house just to get away from me.

She finally told me she's not used to the new guy, this new me. She doesn't know how to act with the new guy. She said that I'm totally different, and she said that when the kids went that summer—because normally the kids go back up to Maryland every summer to visit our family— "I'm going to be at my mom's house for the summer. I've got to really think this out."

I found a letter that she had written, about why she didn't think our relationship was going to work out. I remember she wasn't home, but I called her, and we got together, and I asked her if she still loved me?

She said, "Yeah, but this new guy, I'm not ready for it."

I asked, "Do you want to get to know Jesus?"

"Yeah, but I'm not there where you're at."

I said, "It's okay; everyone's on their own level, but as long as you're willing to try, we'll try Him together."

I tried my best not to talk about Him around her, but it was hard because it just became a part of me. The truth is in the pudding now. We worked it out and built a new life together. The Lord's got so much work for her now, she became a preacher.

She came a long way, but it was really hard. That's what the enemy does. He tries to cause division in the house so the plan of God won't come to pass. I thank God because she hung in there with me, but it was tough. Do we still have struggles? Yeah, we do, but it's really good now for the simple fact that her mind is made up and the Lord Jesus is on our side.

What if the LORD had not been on our side when people attacked us? They would have swallowed us alive in their burning anger. The waters would have engulfed us; a torrent would have overwhelmed us. Yes, the raging waters of their fury would have overwhelmed our very lives. Praise the LORD, who did not let their teeth tear us apart!
We escaped like a bird from a hunter's trap.
The trap is broken, and we are free!
Our help is from the LORD, who made heaven and earth.
Psalm 124:2-8 NLT

THANK YOU, JESUS!

Back when I was living in the Maryland/DC area, my kids would be with me most of the time. Instead of going to daycare, they would hang with me. I would have them with me when I was selling my dope and running the streets.

Some things I didn't think they knew or remembered, but kids aren't stupid. We joke about it now because I used to tell them I was selling elephant trunks, you know, ivory. And I found out they knew that it was cocaine.

They are really great. My daughter, Sade, she has a calling on her life. The Lord showed me when she was about 13 years old. The Lord showed me her calling. It's starting to come around now. She's starting to believe it now, but at first, she was a party animal, clubbing, everything in the world. I see how the Lord is working with her. My daughter definitely has a relationship with God.

My son, he's a tough cookie there. He loves kids. He worked in a nursery in the church. He works in group home jobs, helping kids and being a probation officer. He lives in Maryland, so he comes to our church sometimes, not as much as I want him to, but they're grown so I don't put pressure on them.

My son, he's quiet, he holds a lot of stuff in, but his faith is in the Lord.

Train up a child in the way he should go, And when he is old he will not depart from it.

Proverbs 22:6 NKJV

THE LORD TELLS US TO TRAIN THEM AND HE WILL DO THE REST

My kids were fine with my transition because they were really young at the time. The struggle was with my wife. There were times when the kids and I would go to church and she wouldn't go. And that's understandable because when it's one person here and another person over there, it's hard to get that balance. It's good that the children were a bridge between us. That's truly a blessing.

I love pastoring! I mean, I live for it. I didn't know—if I knew back then, I would have said yes to the Lord a long time ago. I love to speak on behalf of the Lord because it's not me, it's Him. I love it. I love when He uses me. He uses me at any given time, it can be in the grocery store, and it doesn't matter. I believe that wherever I go, it's a purpose, ordained, orchestrated by Him. With that type of mindset, I see him doing it. He shows me every time.

The Lord is showing me now that he is going to use me becoming an author as an avenue to reach more people. Not to dwell on the negative but share my testimony on how God is using me.

The Bible tells us to consider challenges as opportunities to grow.

Dear brothers and sisters, when troubles of any kind come
your way, consider it an opportunity for great joy.
For you know that when your faith is tested,
your endurance has a chance to grow.
So let it grow, for when your endurance is fully developed,
you will be perfect and complete, needing nothing.
If you need wisdom, ask our generous God,
and he will give it to you. He will not rebuke you for asking.
James 1:2-5 NLT

Count on joy when you fall into trials and tribulations, because it's the testing of your faith. God wants you to know that all the stuff that happens in the world is just going to strengthen you in the long run. All these things that happen, it's just building you up.

It's like the story of the old goat that fell in the well. The farmer couldn't get the goat out, so he tried to bury it instead. He began to shovel dirt on the goat, but the goat would just shake it off and stomp it, and with each shovel full of dirt it got farther up. We can get out of the deepest wells just by not stopping, never giving up. Shake it off and take a step up.

These things that try you, these adversities that happen in life, they are just going to strengthen you in the long run. It's the testing of your faith, so let it have its perfect work for you to be completely mature. Then, for that reason, you're able to help somebody else who's going through those types of situations as well. Just. Pass. It. On.

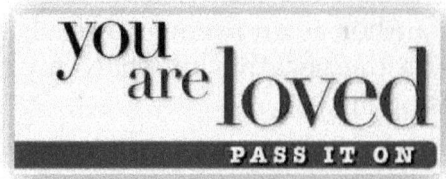

That's what He was telling me there. It's going to be used to encourage people to believe, *If he can make it, I know I can make it.* That's why I have to use Philippians 4:13—"I can do all things"—because we can't do nothing without Him. We may think we are doing something, but it's not to the glory of Him.

> *So Jesus explained, "I tell you the truth, the Son can do nothing by himself. He does only what he sees the Father doing. Whatever the Father does, the Son also does. For the Father loves the Son and shows him everything he is doing. In fact, the Father will show him how to do even greater works than healing this man. Then you will truly be astonished.*
> **John 5:19-20 NLT**

Writing a book has been on my mind and in my heart for at least five years. The Lord had put it in me, and I've been so afraid, fearful even to begin.

When the Lord placed it in me about five years ago to write a book, I was making up excuses and I had some good ones. I can't write. I can't spell. I don't know how to do it. It's going to cost a lot of money. Then, what started to happen is that Bishop George Bloomer told his story about his first book on the Word Network. He said he didn't know how to read or write and the Lord told him that there are people who can record it, transcribe it, and things of that nature. That encouraged me.

In 2011 I started to Google how to write a book. There was this gentleman who started a conversation with me on

Facebook by the name of Brother Adiodun Afolayan. He was a complete stranger, and I had never met him before in my life. He used to message me and ask about my book.

He would ask me, "Have you started on your book?"

He always encouraged and supported me. One day I said, "I've got good news for you."

He asked, "What is it?"

"I've got somebody that's going to help me out with my book."

He was really happy and I told him that I was going to put his name in it to thank him for motivating me.

I see these opportunities that came when I needed assistance, and how God was working it all out for His glory.

I was blessed with Mrs. Ari Squires, an author and business coach who's helped with my book. I was on Facebook one night, and she posted something about how to write a book, and that she had step-by-step guidance on book publishing. She was giving it away to her Facebook friends, and I happened to be one of them. That was another encounter, a God encounter that the Lord was speaking to me again about writing this book.

I remember I had to message her because I didn't have her number at the time, and I shared a little bit with her, and said we have to meet. She felt my urgency and we met that week. I shared what the Lord gave me five years ago, and she was ready to move right away. I thank God for it because this has been building in me so long.

The Bible tells us,

Being confident of this very thing,
that He who has begun a good work in you will complete it
until the day of Jesus Christ.
Philippians 1:6 NKJV

My advice to people is to nurture and grow your dreams, your births, what he put in you, don't keep it dormant. Believe that it is going to come to pass because it will. God will connect you with people that will allow it to come out. You don't have to know everything, but God will have people who know just what you need to carry it through. I thank God for all the people who helped me. I mean, it's been a burden off me. Not fearful now. I have peace of God now.

You will keep him in perfect peace, Whose mind is stayed on You, Because he trusts in You. Trust in the LORD forever, For in YAH, the LORD, is everlasting strength.
Isaiah 26:3-4 NKJV

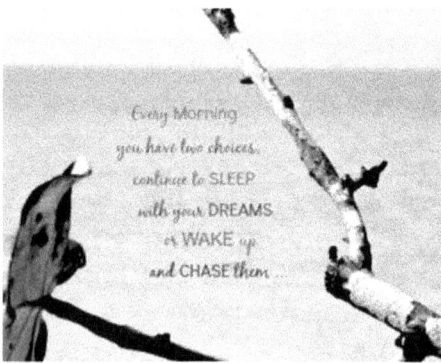

Take a leap in faith and know that God has all the answers that you need. Don't allow the fear to limit you. With God you are limit-less. Take action so you can achieve every dream you have in life. God is just waiting for you to move. Let today be the day.

Faith is the confidence that what we hope for will actually happen; it gives us assurance about things we cannot see.
Hebrews 11:1 NLT

CHAPTER EIGHT

Encounter with God, New Birth

When you encounter God Himself, you will never be the same.
—Timothy Jackson, Pastor, Trinity Fellowship International Church

YOU HAVE TO EXPERIENCE HIM FOR YOURSELF

I used to hear people talk about this God, this Jesus, and Holy Spirit, and I never understood it at all. I thought they were crazy. But when you experience Him you will never be the same. You will grow like a baby, you will change totally from the inside and it starts showing up on the outside.

With Nicodemus in John Chapter 3, he didn't understand at first when he went to Jesus by night. He was saying, "I see that you're a man sent by God because nobody could say or do the things you do. Not unless God was with them."

And Jesus said "You must be born again."

Nicodemus was an old man, and he said, "Surely, I can't go back in the mother's womb."

He didn't comprehend that until he experienced it, it cannot be understood. It's a spiritual new birth; you are born again, born into the family of God. It's like you have this new nature, and the new nature is Christ, and he lives on the inside by the Holy Spirit. And then the Holy Spirit starts teaching you. And like any baby, you've got to nurse that baby, you've got to feed it and give it nutrition and the same thing with the new birth.

*Like newborn babies, you must crave pure spiritual milk
so that you will grow into a full experience of salvation.
Cry out for this nourishment, now that
you have had a taste of the Lord's kindness.*

1 Peter 2:2-3 NLT

You've got to spend time with Jesus. You've got to spend time in the Word and He will start feeding you, and then that baby, that new birth, will start growing and maturing. In that way, you are able to help somebody else.

PASS IT ON!

It's a miracle, that's what it is. It's a miracle! When Jesus really comes into your heart, it's a miracle. It is life changing, and you will never be the same.

I think back to that day at Mt. Zion Baptist Church when I got saved and when I was hearing Jesus speak to me personally. I remember accepting Him, just calling out, telling him, "I need you; I need you now."

Some people say, "I'm a sinner," and that's okay for them, but I was telling Him, "I need you, Lord, I need you, and I need you right now."

When I said that, it's like things that were around me going on and I didn't see it. It wasn't a concern. It's like a peace came over me, a peace that I really can't explain. And it wasn't a feeling, it was just this peace.

*Be anxious for nothing,
but in everything by prayer and supplication,
with thanksgiving, let your requests be made known to God;
and the peace of God, which surpasses all understanding,
will guard your hearts and minds through Christ Jesus.*

Philippians 4:6-7 NKJV

At that point I wasn't worried about anything or anyone. Like an illumination of my thought pattern, everything changed, and He literally came into me. And what I mean by that—and somebody else may explain it differently—I end up the old man dying, and He ends up living His life through me.

As Paul said in the book of Galatians:

I have been crucified with Christ; it is no longer I who live, but Christ lives in me; and the life which I now live in the flesh I live by faith in the Son of God, who loved me and gave Himself for me.
Galatians 2:20 NKJV

So, when He comes and transforms you into his likeness, this new birth, you are no longer yourself anymore. You've begun to allow Him to live through you. You are His ambassador; you are His mouthpiece now.

I preached the sermon years ago, and it was titled, "I'm Not the Same." I took it from the Book of Acts, when Paul had that encounter with God. He kept on kicking against the goads:

Then he fell to the ground, and heard a voice saying to him, "Saul, Saul, why are you persecuting Me?" And he said, "Who are You, Lord?"
Then the Lord said, "I am Jesus, whom you are persecuting. Now get up and go into the city, and you will be told what you must do."
Acts 9:4-5 NIV

It's like that naturally, spiritually, we were blinded for all those years, and then He said, "Receive your sight," and then when you open your eyes, everything looks different. Even though you've got the same hand, the TV is the same, the wall is the same, there is a difference, and really, you have to experience it. You have to experience God to really know Him.

| Message of Inspiration and Hope |

Can you think of a time where God came into your life and spoke a powerful message that even if you tried you couldn't even explain it? Some of us have felt it a long time ago and have either tried to deny it or overlook it. When God speaks, he speaks in a way that only you can receive it. It may be through a story, a passage, an experience or even from the mouth of someone else. However He speaks to you, you will know it because you will feel His spirit run through your body in some type of way. God has a way of making us listen. Find God, know God, and you shall be set free.

For God so loved the world that He gave His only begotten Son, that whoever believes in Him should not perish but have everlasting life.
John 3:16 NKJV

Then Jesus said to those Jews who believed Him, "If you abide in My word, you are My disciples indeed. And you shall know the truth, and the truth shall make you free."
John 8:31-32 NKJV

> **TODAY**
> WILL NEVER COME AGAIN.
> *Be a blessing.*
> *Be a friend.*
> *Encourage someone.*
> Take Time To Care.
> Let your words heal,
> and not wound.

CHAPTER NINE

Speak into Your Life

Don't take it lightly when someone comes and speaks into your life.
—Timothy Jackson, Pastor, Trinity Fellowship International Church

> *Death and life are in the power of the tongue,*
> *And those who love it will eat its fruit.*
> **Proverbs 18:21 NKJV**

There comes a time when God can use anybody to speak into your life. You never know when it's that God-given time for your turn around. For me, it was when Mrs. Stephens sincerely spoke to me about how kind-hearted I was and that she saw great things for me in my future. If you remember, I mentioned I was doing work for her in her basement and she laid hands on me and prayed for me. She told me I was going to be great, but at the time I was struggling so hard to make ends meet I didn't pay her any mind. However, I did listen to her, but that was it. I just listened.

As I look back at it now, that was my turnaround, even though my life changed and I started my own business a little while later, she still spoke that into my life. For her to say what she said, I know without a doubt that God used her for that.

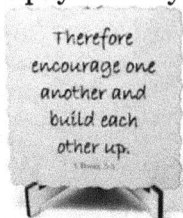

> *Therefore encourage one another and build each other up.*

When I say, "Don't take it lightly when people speak into your life," it's because that one word, or those two words, or that one sentence can change a life forever in a great, positive way.

To be able to bless somebody is to pass it on. I believe that we are on this earth not just for ourselves, but we are on this earth to be a blessing to others in any way or kind of gift that we can. We, in turn, give to others to help them to succeed.

Let each of you look out not only for his own interests,
but also for the interests of others.
Philippians 2:4 NKJV

PLANT SEEDS AND WATCH THEM GROW

The more we plant the seeds, the Bible tells us, we are going to reap a harvest. It talks in Genesis that Isaac was in a famine—meaning nothing was growing—and as he sowed in a famine, the Bible says, he didn't just reap 30-fold or 60-fold, but he reaped 100-fold in that same season. That lets me know that we don't have to allow this world to dictate how we should move and operate because we are under God now.

When Isaac planted his crops that year, he harvested a
hundred times more grain than he planted, for the LORD
blessed him. He became a very rich man, and his wealth
continued to grow.
Genesis 26:12-13 NLT

SOW THE WORD. YOU CAN'T GO WRONG.

By Isaac sowing while things were tough, he ended up getting back more than what he sowed. I believe that as we plant seeds in people (the Word of God), we are going to get back more than what we put out, in some type of way. Whether it's monetary, whether it's material, whatever it is, God will show favor in some way. I just believe that it's important for us to be a blessing for people. Not to say that we are doing it to get a blessing, but that's just the way God works. He's a multiplication type of guy. He wants us to multiply.

> A BLESSING AWAITS THE MAN WHO IS KINDLY, SINCE HE SHARES HIS BREAD WITH THE POOR
> ❀ PROVERBS 22:9 ❀

Again, as we sow seeds—whatever type of seeds they are—the Bible says in the Book of Galatians, "We're going to reap what we sow." As we are going to reap something back, consider what our choices can bring into the world.

CHAPTER TEN

Healed by His Stripes

But He was wounded for our transgressions,
He was bruised for our iniquities;
The chastisement for our peace was upon Him,
And by His stripes we are healed.
Isaiah 53:5 NKJV

In 2003, I was working on the job and kept coughing real bad and didn't know what was happening. Believe it or not, I felt like, *"I've got so much I have got to do, and I can't go to the doctor even though my wife has insurance. I can't afford to go."*

In other words, I couldn't stop working. I had so many jobs at the time. So, I kept working and I kept coughing. It got to the point where it got so bad I had to actually lay down on the job in the basement we were working on. My team kept trying to get me to go to the doctor, but I wouldn't.

The client came down because she heard me. She was a believer so she prayed for me and said, "You're going to go to the doctor right now."

My plan was to go that day, but I never did. I just said, "Let me get out of her house."

It was raining that day, and I kept coughing. I had this extremely bad cough where you can't catch your breath. I told the guy I was riding with to pull the car over. He pulled over and I got out of the truck and started coughing real badly where I couldn't catch my breath.

He said my knees had buckled and I was about to fall out. I coughed so loud that the people in the houses nearby heard me. A woman came out of her house and asked me did I want her to call 911.

I said, "No, let's get back in the car."

I made it home and my wife said, "Are you going to be okay?"

"Yeah, I'm going to be okay." She tried to get me to go to the hospital, but I said, "No, I've got to take care of these jobs and all that over my health."

Finally, it got to the point where it was so bad that I couldn't even take four steps without getting out of breath, so I finally said, "Yeah, I'm going to go to the doctor."

My wife was at work, and I went in. I didn't call her until they admitted me.

First, they did an X-ray, and didn't find anything. They didn't know what was going on. So, they sent me home. One or two days later, the Lord told me to go back and do a CT scan.

I called my doctor and asked if he could refer me to get a CT scan. He set that up, and my wife went with me. I told them why I was there, and what happened, and they did the CT scan with the dye, and they have to look at the X-ray before you go.

They didn't let me leave. They said, "We're going to have to keep you. This doesn't look too good."

I was admitted that day. They hooked me up with prednisone and other medicines. Then, my pulmonary doctor came in the next day and told me what was happening. I had a hole in my lung, and it was probably from coughing. I didn't know you could blow a hole in your lung from coughing so much, but there was a hole in my lung.

They had to do a chest tube operation where they inflate it back up. They set me up and I had it done.

They said, "In two to three days you would be back home."

Good. But it didn't work out like that. I ended up being there for over 30 days.

I was weighing 320 at the time and went down to 256 within a little over 30 days. I was quarantined because they thought I had tuberculosis. The staff thought I was going to die, when they came to check on me they always had something negative to say.

When they introduced me to a new surgeon he said, "We're going to have to operate. I don't want to, but it's serious. We've got to operate."

I kept on praying to the Lord, "No, Lord I don't want this to happen."

I remember trying to turn over to that little table with the wheels on it, and I had a cup of water. I couldn't turn over, I couldn't reach it. I could only look at it.

The Lord said to me, "See, how you're here and you can't do anything. You can't touch this, you can't get that. You can't do nothing without me, son."

When he said that, I knew what he was talking about. Again I had started to do the job and forgot about Him.

I told him, "If you get me out of this—*ha, you always say that*—if you get me out of this one Lord, I promise you I'm going to give my all to you. I promise."

Every problem is an opportunity to trust God

The Lord came through for me, and I didn't have to have an operation. The hole healed up, and the infection went away. I was released from the hospital.

My wife didn't tell me this when I was in the hospital, but she said later that it looked like I was really near death. She couldn't tell me then, of course, but told me when I got better.

Something similar happened in 2012. This time I reacted within two weeks—I'm a little hardheaded. I finally went to the doctor, and I had pneumonia and didn't even know it.

They said I had had it for a while and it was a bad infection. They put me on a breathing machine and did tests, and found a hole in another part of my lungs. The hospital had the technology to use a robot to operate, but the specialist was wary to use it.

He said, "It's way too risky. We definitely don't want to do it. We're not going to do it."

All that could be done was to keep me safe and let me get better.

I met a few good people while I was there. One of the nurses talked with me about the Lord, and she would say, "We get problem people, but you're so nice. We ask you if you need anything and you say no."

After two weeks I was discharged and sent home to continue to recover.

They told me I couldn't lift 10 pounds. They told me not to cough or I might put another hole in my lung. I was scared and asked myself, *Wow, I've got this hole, what's going to happen?*

While I was in there, the Lord gave me a sermon, and the sermon was about faith. Ironically, I wasn't able to physically give the sermon in our church without help.

For assuredly, I say to you, whoever says to this mountain, 'Be removed and be cast into the sea,' and does not doubt in his heart, but believes that those things he says will be done, he will have whatever he says. Therefore I say to you, whatever things you ask when you pray, believe that you receive them, and you will have them.

Mark 11:23-24 NKJV

The Lord had me study about the five biggest mountains to climb. I read about how many miles high each mountain was, and similar facts. I asked the nurse to come to our church, if she didn't mind, and help me do this sermon that the Lord gave me. A month later she came and read about these different mountains and how high they are. What we said was that regardless of the mountains in your life—regardless how big they may look—your faith can be as small as a mustard seed, and you can still tell that thing that it has to go.

I had my two CT scans—the one when I was admitted to the hospital with a hole in my lung, and a second scan taken a month later. The Lord healed me, and I showed everyone in the congregation. I had her to be a witness.

BY MY STRENGTH YOU ARE HEALED

JESUS DIDN'T JUST SAVE MY LIFE HE MADE MY LIFE WORTH SAVING

Before I went to get the second CT scan the Lord spoke to me and told me, "By My strength you are healed."

I went there with confidence knowing that I'm healed. Then, when I found out that it was closed, the Lord reminded me what he said. The test results just proved my faith in the Lord.

And Saul said to David, "You are not able to go against this Philistine to fight with him; for you are a youth, and he a man of war from his youth."
But David said to Saul, "Your servant used to keep his father's sheep, and when a lion or a bear came and took a lamb out of the flock, I went out after it and struck it, and delivered the lamb from its mouth; and when it arose against me, I caught it by its beard, and struck and killed it. Your servant has killed both lion and bear; and this uncircumcised Philistine will be like one of them, seeing he has defied the armies of the living God."
Moreover David said, "The LORD, who delivered me from the paw of the lion and from the paw of the bear, He will deliver me from the hand of this Philistine."
And Saul said to David, "Go, and the LORD be with you!"
1 Samuel 17:33-37 NKJV

DON'T ALLOW PEOPLE TO TALK YOU OUT OF WHAT GOD HAS DONE AND IS DOING IN YOUR LIFE

David looked back on some past experiences where God helped him. His faith gave him confidence to keep going forward.

Have confidence in God. Just look back on when God was there.

God says in Isaiah 41:10, "Don't be afraid, because I am with you. Don't be intimidated; I am your God. I will strengthen you. I will help you. I will support you with my victorious right hand."

He is there to help us. He is there to strengthen us, regardless of what situation we get into. I'm finally at that

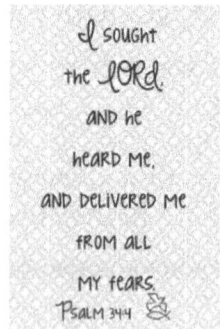

I sought the LORD, and he heard me, and delivered me from all my fears. Psalm 34:4

70

point that I believe that whatever comes my way now, I'm going to have the confidence to know that God's got me.

Once you've experienced Him time and time again, it builds up your confidence—not in you, but it builds up your confidence in Him. He will always show you where He is apt to help you on everything.

I will **WALK BY FAITH** *even when I can not see* Regardless of age, color, or where you came from, there may be some limitations that you have put on yourself, or that the world has put on you, or even some limitations that the devil may have put on you to tell you what you cannot do.

Don't allow any of that to stop you.

As the Bible says in Philippians 4:13: "I can do all things through Christ Jesus who strengthens me."

This lets us know that we can do whatever God put in our heart to do through his power.

All of my experiences that I have been through, good and bad, I wouldn't take any of it back because they have all made me who I am today in Christ.

If you are going through any similar situation, my advice is to hang in there. It's going to get better. You have to have faith in Jesus the Christ. He's the one who makes everything possible. If He can do it for me, someone who came from the ghetto of Washington, DC, and raise me up to someone to have a spiritual and sound mind, he can do the same for you.

Love the Lord with all your heart, your mind, your soul—your everything. Just love him with all your being and all that's in you. Just love Him.

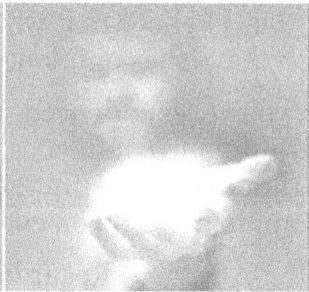

About the Author

Pastor Timothy Jackson was born and raised in Washington, DC. He accepted the Lord Jesus Christ and was baptized at Mount Zion Baptist Church in Spotsylvania, VA, in June 1995. He is married to the former Sandra Wright. They have two children, Sade and Timothy Jr.

Pastor Jackson received the call to preach the gospel in March 2000. Being obedient to the Lord's call, he was licensed that year and later ordained in 2005 by his father in the ministry, Pastor Charles Wormley of Mount Zion Baptist Church. Under Pastor Wormley's tutelage, Pastor Tim enrolled in the Fredericksburg Bible Institute and Seminary and received his associate degree in biblical studies. He is presently pursuing his bachelor's in religious education.

Timothy Jackson is the founding pastor of Trinity South & Trinity North. He has a deep passion for leading people into an intimate relationship with God.